The Essence of Machiavelli's
The Prince

The Essence of Machiavelli's
The Prince

Edited with an Introduction by
Carlo Celli

Revised and updated version
of an original translation by
W. K. Marriott

Letter from Niccolò Machiavelli
to Francesco Vettori translated by
Carlo Celli

AXIOS

The Essence of . . . series of books are edited versions
of great works of moral philosophy, distilled to reveal
the essence of their authors' thought and argument.
To read the complete, unedited version of this work,
and see the excised passages, please visit our website at
www.AxiosPress.com.

Axios Press
P.O. Box 118
Mount Jackson, VA 22842
888.542.9467   info@axiospress.com

Library of Congress Cataloging-in-Publication Data

   The essence of Machiavelli's the Prince / edited with an introduction by Carlo Celli.
   p. cm.
   Includes index.
   ISBN 978-1-60419-043-4 (pbk.)
   1. Political science—Italy—History—16th century 2. Machiavelli,
Niccolò, 1469–1527. I. Celli, Carlo, 1963– II. Machiavelli, Niccolò,
1469–1527. Principe. English. Selections.

JC143.M4E87 2011

320.1–dc22

                                                    2010052405

Contents

Introduction

NICCOLÒ MACHIAVELLI (1469–1527), civil servant and author, was born into a noble but not especially wealthy Florentine family on May 3, 1469, the same year that Lorenzo de' Medici ("The Magnificent") took power in Florence, attempting to retain a de facto hereditary duchy in a city with a long republican tradition.

The Italy of Machiavelli's youth benefited from relative political stability and the balance of power between the major city-states (Venice, Milan, Florence, Naples, and the papacy in Rome) that fostered the artistic, cultural, and economic achievements of the Italian Renaissance. By the time Machiavelli was an adult, the idyll had been broken by the Italian Wars (1494–1534), which began with the invasion by King Charles VIII of France. The consolidated monarchies of Europe (i.e., Spain and France) fought for Continental hegemony, with the Italian city-states as pawns in the conflict.

The late 15th and early 16th centuries was also a period of tremendous cultural change, with the first real diffusion of printed books in Italy in the 1460s, the challenge to the papacy from the Protestant Reformation beginning in 1517, and tensions between competing political, cultural, and religious ideologies of Christian fundamentalism, classical Epicureanism, and republicanism versus monarchic absolutism.

The Florence of Machiavelli's youth had witnessed the rediscovery of classical culture at the court of Lorenzo the Magnificent. After Lorenzo's death in 1492, there was a fundamentalist backlash as the city reestablished a republican government under the influence of the charismatic Dominican friar Girolamo Savonarola (1452–1498), who saw the invasion by Charles VIII as divine retribution for the sins of Italy's rulers, including the pope.

After Savonarola was excommunicated, tried, and burned at the stake in 1498, Machiavelli gained a position in the chancery of the Florentine republic. As a functionary in the Florentine republic, Machiavelli experienced first hand the difficulties of Italian city-states like Florence striving to maintain autonomy under continuing incursions by the consolidated European monarchies. Machiavelli actively participated in diplomatic missions throughout Italy, France, and Germany, and interacted with the main political figures of the period, including Cesare Borgia (1475/76–1507), the ruthless, illegitimate son of Pope Alexander VI. Borgia was intent on using the fluidity of the political and military situation to carve out a personal fiefdom in central Italy.

Machiavelli's political career terminated in 1512, when the Medici regained power in Florence, ending the republic and reestablishing themselves as lords of the city. Some of the blame for the fall of the Florentine republic lay squarely with Machiavelli, who had organized the citizen militia routed by Spanish troops in Prato in 1512. The militia had not been favored by the Florentine nobility, who feared it more than any foreign power. The debates regarding Machiavelli's militia give an idea of his tenuous position in Florentine society, as his family's meager patrimony excluded them from the Florentine elite. Following the Medici restoration of 1512, Machiavelli found himself suspected of participating in an anti-Medici plot and suffered a harrowing stint in prison, where torture sessions included being hauled by a rope with his hands tied behind his back, risking the dislocation of his shoulders. Machiavelli was freed under an amnesty following the election of Giovanni de' Medici as Pope Leo X in 1513.

With the Papal States ruled by a Medici pope, the clan controlled most of central Italy. A main theme in *The Prince* is Machiavelli's hope that the Medici would take advantage of their good fortune to revive the ancient glory of the peninsula and unify Italy under their rule. *The Prince* ends with a citation of Francesco Petrarch's poem *All'Italia* inciting Italians to rid the peninsula of barbarians and reclaim the glory of ancient Rome.

In an obvious attempt to demonstrate his skill as political advisor and regain employment, Machiavelli dedicated *The Prince* to the head of the Medici clan in Florence, Lorenzo de' Medici (1492–1519), grandson of the more renowned Lorenzo "the Magnificent," but there is no evidence that any Medici prince actually ever read the work, and Machiavelli's republican past effectively blacklisted him from service in the regime.

Francesco Guicciardini (1483–1540), Machiavelli's friend and the foremost Italian historian of the period, was the chief advisor to a second Medici pope, Clement VII (1478–1534). Guicciardini was able to assign Machiavelli to some missions before 1527, the year of Machiavelli's death—as well as the year of the cataclysmic Sack of Rome by the Spanish Imperial forces of Charles V, an event interpreted by Guicciardini as vindication of Savonarola's prophesies of divine retribution for the sins of Italy's princes. An important theme in *The Prince* is that the sins of Italy's rulers were not just personal or moral but above all political, for the error of their ways allowed the foreign subjugation of Italy.

Between the fall of the Florentine republic and his death in 1527, Machiavelli dedicated himself to literary pursuits, composing poetry, comedies such as *The Mandrake* (still performed today), and histories in the tradition of those written by civil servants of the Florentine republic. Only one of his works, *The Art of War* (1521), was actually published during his lifetime.

The Prince was eventually published in 1532 and subsequently placed on the papal index of prohibited books. Its diffusion in northern Europe gained Machiavelli notoriety as the source for ideas of moral expediency for political and personal gain. In Elizabethan England, "Old Nick" became a synonym for the devil. Machiavelli's negative reputation grew in the anti-Italian climate in France during the regency of Catherine de' Medici. The general conception of Machiavelli is as the originator of the idea that "the ends justify the means" (although this is never stated directly in *The Prince*), and "Machiavellian" has become synonymous with the use of cunning and deception for personal or political gain.

Over the centuries, some of Machiavelli's most attentive readers have been confirmed despots who certainly applied Machiavellian methods in their careers. However, many other writers and philosophers, before and since, have made openly "Machiavellian" arguments rationalizing immoral or amoral acts for the attainment of a desired goal. One could even argue that there is a Machiavellian essence to any government policy, since the threat of legitimized force in any state achieves its aims. So the question arises, why is the idea of the acceptance and promotion of moral expediency to obtain a desired result so identified with Machiavelli and his short treatise of advice to rulers, *The Prince*? What is it about *The Prince* that has made it one of the fundamental texts in Western civilization for more than five centuries?

Machiavelli equates the prince's life and personal power with the survival of the state. Because the emphasis of Machiavelli's advice is applicable to individuals, his book has appealed not only to princes but also to anyone interested in increasing their influence and standing.

There was an established genre of advice books to princes in prior centuries by authors who, like Machiavelli, hoped to find employment at the court of a prince. What separates *The Prince* from the crowd is its almost ruthless content and direct, discursive style. Machiavelli's advice is brutally straightforward with chapter titles like "Concerning Those Who Have Obtained a Principality through Wickedness." Rarely in *The Prince* does Machiavelli tiptoe in an effort to avoid giving offense. The result is as refreshingly realistic today as half a millennium ago.

———— ❦ ————

In *The Prince* Machiavelli concentrates on the extremes in human nature and behavior, describing a naturalistic worldview that owes much to the Roman philosopher Lucretius (99–55 BCE). There is evidence that as a young man Machiavelli made a transcription of Lucretius's *De rerum natura* (*On the Nature of Things*). Much of the realism and materialism in *The Prince* recalls the Epicurean philosopher or at least a common interpretation of him: e.g., Machiavelli's skepticism concerning, if not outright rejection of, ethical concerns and religion, and an emphasis on the fluidity and unpredictability of the cruel forces of nature, which he believes explain not only natural phenomena but also human behavior. To this Lucretian materialism Machiavelli brings his own deep roots in a very local, bawdy Tuscan culture, perhaps most evident in his poems and his comedies but also apparent in his folksy aphorisms about foxes, lions, floods, mud, and storms. The sum of this combination of Lucretian materialism and an archaic Tuscan naturalism is constant regeneration and renewal. Machiavelli teaches not just a realistic acceptance and promotion of moral expediency as a factor in human behavior, but also the importance of a dynamic extremism and radicalism as a permanent condition of life under the caprices of an indifferent and cruel natural world.

When Machiavelli explains in his dedication that to understand a prince one must be of the people (and conversely, to understand the people one must be a prince), he describes an interpretation of the world as a continuous play of contrasts. In Machiavelli, extremism is preferred to moderation—a clear rejection of the Aristotelian ideal of the golden mean. Machiavelli's view of history, with a debt to ancient Greek historians like Polybius, is as a never-ending natural cycle where everything is potentially ruled by and transformed into its opposite in an echo of Lucretius. The historical examples of leaders in *The Prince* become temporary, carnivalesque figures whose sacrificial role is to regenerate the body politic for the greater goal of Italian peninsular power under a Medici prince advised by Machiavelli.*

❧

The present volume provides the essence of Machiavelli's reasoning in *The Prince*. Some sections of the work detailing historical examples have been deleted to allow Machiavelli's philosophy to shine through.

---

* See Carlo Celli, *Il carnevale di Machiavelli* (Florence: Leo S. Olschki Editori, 2009).

Also included is a letter Machiavelli wrote to Francesco Vettori, one of his few friends from his days in the Florentine chancery, to obtain a commission under the Medici. This letter, which describes Machiavelli's hopes to gain a position in the Medici regime by composing *The Prince*, provides insight into Machiavelli's character. The letter is divided between descriptions of bawdy, rustic local life and themes of high erudition. The contrast between a day spent catching thrushes with birdlime and playing cards at the local tavern, and his transformation into a man of letters taking solemn refuge in his study, graphically illustrates Machiavelli's personality as well as his worldview.

—Carlo Celli

Dedication

Niccolò machiavelli to the Magnificent Lorenzo II de' Medici:*

Those who strive to enter into the good graces of a prince are accustomed to come before him with what they value most, or with what they see him as delighting in most; thus princes are often presented with horses, arms, cloth of gold, precious stones, and similar ornaments worthy of their grandeur.

Desiring, therefore, to present myself to your Magnificence with some testimony of my devotion to you, I have found nothing among my possessions that I hold more dear than, or value as much as, the knowledge of the actions of great men, acquired through long experience in current events, and a continuous

---

* The dedication is to Lorenzo di Piero de' Medici (1492–1519), grandson of Lorenzo "the Magnificent" de' Medici (1449–1492).

study of the past. After having long studied and diligently examined these things, I have now condensed them into a little volume that I send to your Magnificence.

And although I may consider this work unworthy to be presented as a gift, nevertheless I trust in your humanity that it may be well received, considering that it is not possible for me to make a better gift than to offer the opportunity to understand in the shortest time everything I have learned in so many years, and with so many troubles and dangers. I have not embellished it with rhetorical phrases or fancy and magnificent words, nor with any affectations or superfluous decoration, as many do. For I wish for nothing to adorn it or to make it pleasing other than the pithiness of the subject and the importance of the theme. Nor do I wish it to be thought presumptuous for a man of low and humble station to dare discuss and provide rules for the governing of princes. Just as those who paint landscapes go down to the plains in order to consider the nature of the mountains and lofty places, and up into the mountains in order to consider the nature of the plains, similarly to completely understand the nature of the people one must be a prince; and to completely understand princes, one must be of the people.

Chapter Three

MEN CHANGE RULERS willingly in the belief they will better themselves. This belief induces them to take up arms against their present ruler: wherein they are deceived, because afterward they will see from experience that things are worse.

Newly acquired states added to a formerly existing state, are either of the same region and language or not. When they are, it is quite simple to retain them, especially if they are not used to living in freedom.* To hold them securely it is enough to have extinguished the line of the ruling prince. If previous conditions can be retained and there are no dissimilarities in customs, men can live quietly.

---

* Machiavelli's term, *vivere liberi*, also has the connotation of self-rule, not subject to a foreign government.

Although there may be some difference in language, nevertheless when customs are alike the people can easily behave themselves. He who has annexed them, if he wants to retain them, has only to bear in mind two considerations: first, that the bloodline of their former prince is extinguished; second, that neither their laws nor taxes are altered, so that in a very short time they will become entirely one body with the old principality.

But when states are acquired in a country differing in language, customs, or institutions, there are difficulties, and good fortune and great industry are needed to retain them. One of the best and most efficient solutions is for the person who has acquired them to go and reside there. Because, being there, one sees disorders as they form, and can soon remedy them; but if one is not there, problems are understood only when they are overwhelming and no longer have a solution. Furthermore the country will not be pillaged by your officials and the subjects will be satisfied by ready access to the prince. They will have more cause to love him if they want to be good and more cause to fear him if they want to behave otherwise. Anyone wanting to attack that state from outside would hesitate; for it will be very difficult for the prince residing there to lose it.

The other better solution is to send colonies to one or two places, to act almost like shackles on that state, for it is necessary either to do this or else to maintain them with many men at arms and infantry. There is not much expense with colonies, for with little or no expense of one's own they can be sent out and held, offending only those from whom fields and houses are taken to be given to the new inhabitants. Those he offends, remaining scattered and poor, will never be able to hurt him. The rest are easily kept quiet and remain calm since they were not harmed nor injured. They will also be hesitant about making any mistakes out of fear that what happened to the despoiled could happen to them. Let me conclude that these colonies are not costly, are more faithful and are not problematic; on the other hand those who were injured can do little harm since they are poor and scattered.

For it must be noted that men should either be well treated or crushed; because they can avenge themselves of light injuries but not more serious ones. Therefore any injury done to a man should be such that one does not fear a vendetta for it.

Whoever is in a province that is different must also make himself the leader and defender of less powerful neighbors, and strive to weaken the more powerful amongst them, taking care that no foreigner as powerful as himself shall, by some circumstance, gain entry there. It always happens that a foreigner will be called in by those who are unhappy either due to excess ambition or fear.

The usual course of affairs is that, as soon as a powerful foreigner enters a country, all the subject states are drawn to him, moved by the resentment they feel against the former ruling power. With respect to those subject states, the foreigner need take no trouble to win them over, for all of them will quickly rally to the state he has acquired there. He has only to be careful that they do not get hold of too much power and too much authority. Then, with his own forces and with their goodwill, he can easily suppress the more powerful of them, so as to remain entirely in control of the country. He who does not properly manage this business will soon lose what he has acquired; and will have endless difficulties and troubles while he holds it.

The Romans did what all prudent princes should do by using all resources at their disposal to counter future as well as present troubles. When problems are anticipated, they are easily remedied; but if you wait until they are pressing, then the medicine will be too late because the disease will have become incurable. What happens is akin to what physicians say about consumption: in the beginning the illness is easy to cure but difficult to diagnose, but over time, if undiagnosed and left untreated, it becomes easy to diagnose but difficult to cure. This also applies to affairs of state: if troubles are detected early, then they can be quickly redressed; but when they remain undetected, they will be left to grow to the point where everyone is aware of them and there is no longer a remedy. Therefore, the Romans always overcame difficulties because they anticipated them and would not let them develop in an effort to avoid a war, because they understood that war cannot be eliminated but only delayed to the advantage of others. They never liked what nowadays continuously comes out of the mouths of wise men—to enjoy the benefits of biding one's time—instead they relied on their own ability and wisdom, because time flushes out everything bringing the good with the bad as well as the bad with the good.

The desire to acquire is quite natural and common, and men will always do so when they can; and they will be praised, not criticized for it. However, when they cannot but want to anyway, here is the error and the blame.

When Cardinal Rouen observed to me that the Italians do not understand war, I replied to him that the French do not understand statecraft, for if they did, they would never have allowed the Church to attain such power.* From experience it may be seen that the power of the Church and of Spain in Italy has been caused by France, whose downfall may be

---

* Cardinal of Rouen Georges d'Amboise (1460–1510). The word translated here and in the text as "power" is *grandezza*, which also has the connotation of prestige and grandeur.

attributed to them. From this a general rule may be drawn that never or rarely fails: whoever causes another to become powerful is ruined, because that predominance has been brought about either by industry or by force, and both are suspect to the one who has become powerful.

Chapter Four

IN KINGDOMS GOVERNED as France is, one can easily enter by winning over some baron of the kingdom, for one always finds malcontents and others who desire change. Such men, for the reasons given, can open the way into the state and facilitate victory; but if you wish to hold it afterwards, you meet with infinite difficulties, both from those who have assisted you and from those you have defeated. Nor is it enough for you to have exterminated the bloodline of the prince, because the lords who remain can make themselves the leaders of new revolutions, and since you can neither satisfy nor exterminate them, you will lose that state at the first occasion.

Chapter Five

WHENEVER THOSE STATES which have been acquired as described have been accustomed to live under their own laws and in freedom, there are three courses for those who wish to hold them: the first is to destroy them; the next is to reside there in person; the third is to permit them to live under their own laws but pay a tribute, and create an oligarchic state that keeps them friendly to you. Such a government, being created by the prince and knowing that it cannot stand without his friendship and interest, does its utmost to support him. It is easier to hold a city accustomed to freedom by means of its own citizens than in any other way, if one wants to preserve it.

He who becomes master of a city accustomed to freedom and does not destroy it may expect to be destroyed by it, for the call of liberty and its ancient

orders have always been a rallying point for rebellion, which neither time nor benefits will ever erase.
And no matter what one may do or prepare for, they
will never forget that name or those rights unless the
inhabitants become disunited or are dispersed. For at
every chance they will rally immediately, as Pisa did
after the hundred years she had been held in bondage
by the Florentines.*

But when cities or countries are accustomed to live
under a prince, and his bloodline is exterminated,
since on the one hand they are accustomed to obey-
ing and on the other hand they no longer have the old
prince; they will not be able to make one from among
themselves and they do not know how to live under
liberty. For these reasons they are very slow to take up
arms and a prince will be able to win them over and
be certain of their loyalty. But republics retain more
vitality, more hatred, and more desire for vengeance.
They will not allow the memory of their former liberty to be put to rest. Therefore, the safest way is to
destroy them or to reside there.

---

* Pisa became a subject of Florence in 1406 and rebelled in 1494 during
the invasion by Charles VIII of France. Florence reconquered Pisa in
1509 with Machiavelli among those at the surrender negotiations.

Chapter Six

THERE IS NOTHING more difficult to handle, more uncertain of success or more dangerous than to take the lead in the introduction of a new order, because the innovator has for enemies all those who did well under the old order, and lukewarm defenders in those who may do well under the new one. This coolness arises partly from fear of opponents who have the law on their side, and partly from the skepticism of men, who do not readily believe in innovation without actually experiencing it. Thus it happens that whenever the opposition has the opportunity to attack, they do so zealously, while the others will defend halfheartedly, so that it is dangerous to remain with them.

If we desire to discuss this matter further, it is necessary to examine whether these innovators can rely on themselves or must depend on others: that is to say, whether in order to carry out their plans they must beg or use force? In the first instance they will always end badly and never accomplish anything; but when they can rely on themselves and use force, they will rarely be in peril. That is why all armed prophets have won, and unarmed ones have been ruined.*

Besides the reasons mentioned, this is because the people are fickle by nature. They are easy to persuade, but it is difficult to hold them to that persuasion. And if they no longer believe, one must be prepared to make them believe by force.

---

* A reference to Girolamo Savonarola (1452–1498), Dominican friar and fundamentalist reformer, whose apocalyptic sermons greatly influenced Florentine politics from the expulsion of the Medici regime in 1494 to his excommunication by pope Alexander VI. Savonarola was tried, hung, and burned at the stake in 1498. Machiavelli's entry into the chancery of the Florentine republic followed the fall of Savonarola and his party.

Chapter Seven

THOSE WHO BECOME princes solely by good fortune after having been private citizens take little effort to rise but much to maintain their new position. They do not have any difficulty on the way up, since they fly there, for all the problems arise once they are in place.

Such men simply rely on two very inconstant and unstable things: the goodwill and the fortune of those who gave them everything. They do not know how to retain their position unless they are men of great worth and ability. It is unreasonable to expect them to know how to rule because they always lived in private life. They are unable because they do not have forces that can remain friendly and reliable.

States that rise unexpectedly—like all other things in nature that are born and grow rapidly—cannot have roots and branches of their own, and so they are destroyed by the first adverse spell; unless, as is said, those who become princes quickly are men of such ability that they immediately understand how to maintain what Fortune placed on their laps, and afterward lay their foundations as others did before becoming princes.

Concerning these two methods of rising to be a prince—by ability or fortune—I wish to offer two examples within our own recollection: Francesco Sforza and Cesare Borgia.* Francesco, by appropriate means and with great ability, rose from being a private person to become the duke of Milan, and what he acquired after a thousand difficulties he kept with little effort. On the other hand, Cesare Borgia, whom the people call Duke Valentino, acquired his state through the fortunes of his father, and lost it in the same way, despite taking every precaution and doing everything a prudent and skillful man could do to put down roots in the states that the arms and fortune of others had bestowed upon him. I do not know what better teachings to give a new prince than the example of his actions. If he did not succeed in his aims, it was not his fault, but the extraordinary and extreme malice of fortune.

---

* Francesco Sforza (1401–1466), military leader and duke of Milan. Cesare Borgia (1475/76–1507), illegitimate son of Pope Alexander VI (1431–1503). Machiavelli observed Borgia's methods while on diplomatic missions for the Florentine Republic.

When he [Cesare Borgia] turned to deceit, he was so able to conceal his intentions that even the Orsini* were reconciled to him through Signor Paolo, whom the Duke did not fail to reassure with every sort of courtesy, giving him money, apparel, and horses. Their foolishness brought them into his power at Senigallia.† Having exterminated these leaders, and having turned their allies into his friends, the Duke laid very good foundations for his power, by having all the Romagna and the Duchy of Urbino, and especially because it seemed to him that he had gained the support of the Romagna region, and all the people who began to enjoy their well-being.

When the Duke occupied Romagna, he found it under the rule of incompetent lords, more ready to steal from their subjects than to rule them, creating more cause for disunity than for unity, so that the country was full of robberies, quarrels, and every sort of insolence. In order to make it peaceful and obedient to authority, he decided it needed a good government. Thereupon, he placed Messer Remirro de Orco in command, giving this cruel and efficient man full authority. In a short time this man brought peace and unity earning a great reputation. Afterward Borgia

---

* The Orsini and Colonna were powerful Roman clans and obstacles to the attempts by Pope Alexander VI and Cesare Borgia to increase the temporal power of the Papacy.

† The "Senigallia massacre" of December 31, 1502.

decided that such excessive authority was no longer required, for he was concerned that it might cause hatred, so he set up a civil court in the center of the province, under a well-qualified president, wherein every city had its own representative. And because he realized that the past severity had generated some hatred, in order to cleanse the spirits of the people and to win them over entirely, he wanted to show that any cruelty practiced did not originate with him but in the harsh disposition of the minister. Under this pretense one morning he had Remirro put in the square at Cesena, cut in two pieces with a block of wood and a bloody knife at his side. The ferocity of this spectacle caused the people to be at once satisfied and amazed.

Such was Borgia's line of action concerning present affairs. But as to the future, he had to fear, in the first place, that a successor to the papacy might not be friendly to him and might seek to take from him what [his father Pope] Alexander had given him. So he decided to secure his position in four ways: first, eliminate the bloodlines of the lords he had despoiled in order to remove that opportunity from the pope; second, win over to himself all the noblemen of Rome in order to keep the pope in check, as has been observed; third, control as much of the College [of Cardinals] as possible; fourth, acquire so much power before the pope died that he could withstand an initial attack on his own. At Alexander's death, of these four things he had accomplished three and had almost completed the fourth. He had killed as many of the dispossessed lords as he could reach, very few saved themselves; he had won over the Roman gentlemen; and he had a considerable following in the College. As for new conquests, he planned to become master of Tuscany, for he already possessed Perugia and Piombino, and Pisa was under his protection. Since he no longer had to fear the French, he could pounce on Pisa; for the French had already been driven out of the kingdom of Naples by the Spaniards, so that both of them were compelled to buy his friendship. After this, Lucca and Siena would have yielded at once, partly out of hatred and fear of the Florentines; for the Florentines had no countermeasures. If he had succeeded (as he was the year Alexander died), he would have acquired so much power and reputation that he could have stood by himself, and no longer would have depended on the fortunes and forces of others, but solely on his own power and ability.

Alexander died just five years after he had first drawn the sword, leaving his son seriously ill, with only the state of Romagna consolidated between two powerful and hostile armies and the rest up in the air. Yet the Duke was so fierce and capable, and understood so well how to win men over or lose them, and the foundations he had laid in such a short time were so solid, that if those armies had not been upon him, or if he had been in good health, he would have withstood every difficulty. That his foundations were good may be seen from how the Romagna region awaited him for more than a month. Although but half-alive, he remained safe in Rome, for when the Baglioni, the Vitelli, and the Orsini came to Rome, they found nobody willing to oppose him.* If he was not able to make someone he wanted pope, at least it would not be someone he did not want. But if he had been in good health at the death of Alexander, everything would have been easy for him. On the day Julius II† was elected, Borgia told me that he had thought of everything that might occur at the death of his father, and had prepared a remedy for everything, but he had never anticipated that when his father died he would also be about to die.

In reviewing all of the Duke's efforts, I cannot blame him, for it seems to me that he is to be imitated by all those who have risen to power by the fortune or the arms of others. Since he had such a grand spirit and far-reaching aims, he could not have conducted himself otherwise, and his plans were stopped only by the shortness of the life of Alexander and his own illness. Therefore, anyone who deems it necessary to

---

* The Baglioni were a noble clan based in Perugia; the Vitelli were based in Città di Castello and the Orsini in Rome.

† Julius II, Giuliano della Rovere (1443–1513), was elected pope in 1503.

protect himself from enemies in a new principality, to gain friends, to conquer by either force or fraud, to make himself beloved and feared by the people, to be followed and revered by soldiers, to exterminate those who have hurt him or could hurt him, to bring innovation and new ways to an aging order, to be severe and gracious, magnanimous and liberal, to eliminate an unreliable military and to create a new one, to establish friendship with kings and princes so that they provide favors graciously and do harm with trepidation, cannot find a more relevant example than the deeds of this man.

He can only be blamed for the election of Julius II, in whom he made a poor choice, because, as is said, not being able to elect a pope of his own, he could have kept anyone from becoming pope; and he should never have consented to the election of any cardinal whom he had harmed or who had cause to fear him if they became pontiff. Men do harm either out of fear or hatred, and anyone who believes that new benefits will make those high in status forget old affronts is deceiving himself. Erring in this choice caused his ultimate downfall.

Chapter Eight

IN OUR TIMES, during the rule of [Pope] Alexander VI, Oliverotto da Fermo, having been left fatherless as a child years past, was brought up by a maternal uncle named Giovanni Fogliani. In his youth he was sent to enlist in the military under Paolo Vitelli in order to be trained in that profession and attain high military rank. After Paolo died, Oliverotto served under his brother Vitellozzo, and before long, since he was enterprising and vigorous in body and mind, he rose to the command of his troops. But it seemed to him servile to remain among the others, so he resolved to seize Fermo with the consent of the Vitelleschi and the aid of some citizens of Fermo who preferred slavery to liberty for their country. He wrote to Giovanni Fogliani about how he had been away from home for many years and wished to visit him and his city, and also in some way acknowledge his inheritance. Since he wanted his countrymen to see that he had not spent his time in vain and had labored only to gain honor, he wished to arrive with full honors, escorted by a hundred horsemen, friends, and servants. He entreated Giovanni to arrange that he be well received by the people of Fermo, thus honoring not only him but also Giovanni, having been in his charge.

Giovanni did arrange for his nephew to be honorably received by the people of Fermo, even giving him lodgings in his own house. After a few days during which Oliverotto waited and secretly made the plans necessary for his wicked designs, he invited Giovanni Fogliani and the leading citizens of Fermo to a solemn banquet. When the meal and other entertainments customary at such banquets had been consumed, Oliverotto artfully moved the conversation to important discussions about the greatness of Pope Alexander and his son Cesare, and of their enterprises. As Giovanni and the others joined in the discussion, Oliverotto suddenly rose up, explaining that such matters should be discussed in a more private place, and retired into another chamber followed by Giovanni and the rest of the citizens. As soon as they were seated, soldiers emerged from secret hiding places and killed Giovanni and the others. After the homicide, Oliverotto mounted his horse, rode up and down the town, and besieged the palace of the chief magistrate, who out of fear was forced to obey him and to form a government with Oliverotto as prince. Since he had killed anyone who might have been sufficiently upset to harm him, he then consolidated his power with new civil and military ordinances, so that for the year he held the principality, not only was he secure in the city of Fermo, but he became feared by all his neighbors. It would have been difficult to remove him from power had he not allowed himself to be deceived by Cesare Borgia and captured with the Orsini and Vitelli at Senigallia a year after the parricide. He was strangled, together with Vitellozzo, whom he had made his guide in valor and wickedness.

Some may wonder how, after infinite treacheries and cruelties, his like* could live for long, secure in their countries; defend themselves from external enemies; and never be conspired against by their own citizenry. Many others have been unable to hold their states by means of cruelty even in peaceful times, much less in the uncertainty of wartime. I believe this stems from cruelty being either poorly or properly applied. Cruelty is properly applied (if it is possible to speak positively of evil) when done in a single stroke and out of self-preservation, then not persisted upon and used to benefit of the subjects as much as

---

* Machiavelli refers to Agathocles, tyrant of Syracuse (361–289 BCE), who came to power in a manner similar to Oliverotto da Fermo.

possible. Cruelty is poorly applied, even if used sparingly at first, when it grows rather than diminishes over time. Those who practice the first system can find some solutions for their state before both God and men; it is impossible for the others to maintain themselves.

Therefore, in seizing a state a conqueror should closely examine all the offences he needs to inflict, and to do everything in a single stroke so as not to have to recur to them daily. By not repeating them, he can reassure men and win them over by helping them. He, who does otherwise, either out of timidity or from poor advice, will always need to keep a knife in hand, for he will never be able to rely on his subjects, nor can they count on him, owing to the continuous and repeated attacks. Injuries should be inflicted all at once so that, being tasted less, they offend less; benefits should be given little by little, so that their flavor may last longer.

Above all, a prince should live among his people in such a way that no unexpected circumstance, good or bad, makes him change behavior. Necessities arise in times of trouble, when you will not have time to resort to evil; and the good you do will not help, since it will be judged as forced, and you will receive no recognition for it.

Chapter Nine

W**E NOW COME** to the case of a leading citizen becoming the prince of his country not by wickedness or any intolerable violence but by the consent of his fellow citizens.

Nor is skill or fortune altogether necessary to attain it, but rather a lucky shrewdness. I say then that such a principality is obtained either by the consent of the people or by the consent of the elite. In all cities these two distinct parties are found, and from this it arises that the people do not wish to be ruled nor oppressed by the elite, but the elite do wish to rule and oppress the people. In cities these two opposing appetites give birth to one of three results: a principality, liberty, or anarchy.

A principality is created either by the people or by the elite, depending on whether one faction or the other has the opportunity. The elite, seeing they cannot withstand the people, begin to increase the reputation of one of themselves and make him a prince, so that under his shadow they can satisfy their appetites. The people, finding they cannot resist the elite, also increase the reputation of someone and make him a prince in order to be defended under his authority. He who obtains the principality by the assistance of the elite maintains himself with more difficulty than he who arrives with the aid of the people. Since the former finds himself surrounded by many who consider themselves his equals, he can neither rule nor manage them to his liking. But he who attains a principality by popular consent finds himself alone, and has either no one or few around him who are not prepared to obey him.

Furthermore, one cannot honestly satisfy the elite without injuring others, but you can satisfy the people, for they are more honest than the elite, who wish to oppress, while the former want only not to be oppressed. In addition, a prince can never secure himself against a hostile people, being too many, while he can secure himself from the elite, who are few. The worst that a prince may expect from a hostile people is to be abandoned by them. But with the elite as enemies, he not only has to fear abandonment, but also that they will act against him. Since they are more clairvoyant and astute in these affairs, they will always act in time to save themselves and will seek the favor of the side they expect to prevail. Furthermore, the prince must always live with the same people, but he can do well without the same elite, since he can make or break them any day, and make them gain or lose reputation at will.

Anyone who becomes a prince with the support of the common people should keep them friendly, which he can easily do because all they ask of him is not to be oppressed. But someone opposed by the people who becomes a prince with the consent of the elite, must, above all else, try to win the people over. This may easily be done once he takes them under his protection, since men, when treated well by those by whom they expected to be harmed, become more obligated to their benefactor. The people will quickly become more devoted to him than if he had been raised to the principality due to their support.

Let no one reject my opinions with the trite proverb, "He who builds on the people, builds upon the mud." This can be true when a private citizen lays his foundation on the people and then allows himself to believe that the people will free him when he is oppressed by his enemies or by the magistrates. In such cases, he could find himself often deceived, as occurred to the Gracchi* in Rome and to Messer

---

* The Gracchi brothers, Gaius Sempronius (160 or 153?–121 BCE) and Tiberius Sempronius (169 or 164?–133 BCE) were Roman tribunes.

Giorgio Scali* in Florence. But a prince who founds himself on the people and knows how to lead like a man of courage, unperturbed by adversity and does not fail to take precautions, and who, by his resolution and energy, can inspire the people—he will never find himself deceived by them for it will be evident that he laid his foundations well.

Principalities are liable to be in danger when passing from constitutional to dictatorial government. These princes either rule by themselves or through magistrates. In the latter case their position is weaker and less secure because they depend on the goodwill of those citizens appointed as magistrates who, especially in troubled times, can take away the state by disobedience or by acting against him. The prince does not have time in a crisis to seize absolute authority, because the citizens and subjects, accustomed to receiving orders from magistrates, are not ready to obey him during a predicament, and in uncertain times he will always lack men he can trust. Such a prince cannot rely upon what he observes in quiet times, when citizens need the state, because then everyone comes running and makes promises and is ready to die for him, since death is nowhere near. In troubled times, however, when the state needs its citizens, then only a few are to be found. And what

---

* Giorgio Scali, a leader of the Ciompi rebellion (1378) in Florence.

makes this experiment even more dangerous is that it can only be tried once. Therefore, a wise prince should think of a way to make his citizens need him and the state in every circumstance, for then they will always be loyal to him.

Chapter Eleven

IT REMAINS NOW to examine ecclesiastical principalities.

When Alexander VI arrived, he was the first pope ever to demonstrate how a pope could use both money and arms to prevail. With Duke Valentino* as his instrument and using the opportunity afforded by the French invasion, he brought to pass everything I discussed above regarding the actions of the Duke. And although his intention was to make the Duke great rather than the Church, what he really did was to increase the power of the Church, which after his death and the passing of the Duke became the heir to all his labors.

Then came Pope Julius who found the Church powerful, possessing all of Romagna; the barons of

---

* Cesare Borgia was also known as Duke Valentino.

Rome destroyed; and the factions wiped out after being beaten down by Alexander. He also discovered the path still open for a way to accumulate money in a manner never practiced before Alexander's time.* Julius not only continued these ways but added to them, planning to conquer Bologna, to ruin the Venetians, and to drive the French out of Italy. He succeeded in all these enterprises, and what is even more praiseworthy, he did everything to strengthen the Church and not some private individual. He also kept the Orsini and Colonnesi factions within the constrained condition in which he had found them.

His Holiness Pope Leo† has found the Papal States in a most powerful position, and it may be hoped that if his predecessors made it great with arms, he will make it still greater and more venerated with his goodness and infinite other virtues.

---

* The practice of selling indulgences.

† The election of Giovanni di Lorenzo de' Medici (1475–1521) as Pope Leo X in 1513 gave the Medici clan control over most of central Italy. An amnesty following Leo X's election freed Machiavelli from prison after the fall of the Florentine republic.

Chapter Twelve

WE HAVE SAID above how necessary it is for a prince to have his foundations firmly laid, for otherwise out of necessity he will be ruined. The chief foundations of all states, new as well as old or mixed, are good laws and good armies. Because there cannot be good laws where there are not good armies, and where there are good armies there must be good laws; I will leave aside discussion of the law and speak about armies.

The armies with which a prince defends his state are either his own or they are mercenary, auxiliary, or mixed. Mercenaries and auxiliaries are useless and dangerous; anyone who attempts to keep a state founded on mercenary armies will never be stable and secure, for they are disunited, ambitious, without discipline, unfaithful, valiant before friends, cowardly before enemies. They have neither fear of God nor faith in men, and ruin is deferred only as long as attack is delayed; in peacetime you are robbed by them and in wartime by the enemy.

The explanation is that mercenaries have no other passion or reason to stay in the field than a meager salary, which is not enough to make them want to die for you. They are ready enough to be your soldiers as long as you are not at war; but when war comes, they either want to flee or go away. The downfall of Italy has been caused by reliance on mercenary armies for so many years. They did seem to help some profit as long as they could act courageously among themselves, but when the foreigners came the mercenaries showed themselves for what they are. That is how King Charles of France could take Italy with a piece of chalk.* He who told us that our sins were the cause told the truth, but they were not the sins he imagined, rather those which I have related.† And since these were the sins of princes, they have also suffered the penalty.

---

* "With chalk," *col gesso* refers to the ease with which Charles VIII seized Italy, implying that it was only necessary for him to send his quartermasters to chalk up the billets for his soldiers in order to conquer the country.

† Machiavelli refers to the sermons of the charismatic Dominican friar Girolamo Savonarola, who interpreted the French invasions of 1494 as divine retribution for the sins of Italy's rulers, including the pope. For Machiavelli the sins were not just ethical or moral, but practical and political.

Mercenary captains are either excellent military men or they are not; if they are, you cannot trust them, because they always aspire to their own power either by oppressing you, their master, or by oppressing others against your interests. Of course, if the captain has no skill at all, he will ruin you in the normal way.

After Italy fell into the hands of the Church and various republics, because the Church is run by priests and republics run by citizens unaccustomed to arms, both began to hire foreign soldiers.

The end result of all their virtue is that Italy has been overrun by Charles, plundered by Louis, ravaged by Ferdinand, and insulted by the Swiss.* Italy has been left in slavery and shame.

---

* The French kings Charles VIII and Louis XII; and Ferdinand II (1452–1516), king of Aragon and Castile.

Chapter Thirteen

THE OTHER USELESS type of army is the auxiliary army, which is when you request a power to come to your aid and defense with their army. This was done by Pope Julius in recent times when he saw how poorly his mercenaries fared in the Ferrara campaign. He turned to auxiliaries and contracted with king Ferdinand of Spain for assistance with men and arms. These armies may be useful and good in themselves, but they are always damaging to anyone who calls upon them, for in defeat you are undone, in victory you become their prisoner.

Chapter Fourteen

A PRINCE SHOULD HAVE no other aim or thought, nor select anything else for his profession, than war, its rules, and discipline; for the art of war is the only discipline that suits a ruler, and is of such virtue that not only does it maintain those who are born princes, but it often enables men to rise from a private station to that rank. On the other hand, it is evident that when princes pay more attention to refinements than to arms, they lose their states. The first way to lose a state is to neglect the art of war; and the way to acquire one is to be master of this art.

Francesco Sforza went from being a private citizen to the duke of Milan because he was armed. His sons went from being dukes to private citizens because they avoided the hardships and troubles of arms. One of the worst consequences of being unarmed is that it makes you despicable, an infamy against which a prince should be on guard, as will be explained below. There can be no comparison between an armed and an unarmed man. It is unreasonable for an armed man to willingly obey a man who is unarmed, or for an unarmed man to feel safe among armed servants. Since there is disdain in one and suspicion in the other, it is impossible for them to work well together. A prince who does not understand the military, in addition to other problems already mentioned, cannot hold the respect of his soldiers, nor can he rely on them. The subject of war should never leave his thoughts. In peacetime he should dedicate himself even more to it than in wartime. He can do this in two ways; one by action, the other with the mind.

As regards action, besides keeping his men well organized and drilled; he must always go out hunting in order to accustom his body to hardships. He must learn the lay of the land, observing how mountains rise, how valleys extend, and how plains lie. He must understand the nature of rivers and swamps, and do all this with great dedication.

As to the exercise of the mind, the prince must read history and study the actions of illustrious men, to see how they carried themselves in war, and examine the causes of their victories and defeats.

Chapter Fifteen

I T REMAINS NOW to see about the conduct and rules for a prince toward subjects and friends. Since I know that many have written about this; I fear it may be considered presumptuous to write about it again, especially because I shall not follow the methods established by others in discussing the topic.* But since my intention is to write something useful for those capable of understanding, it appears to me more appropriate to follow the actual truth of the matter rather than how it may be imagined. Many have imagined republics and principalities that have never been seen nor experienced in reality. There is such a difference between how one lives and how one ought to live that he who neglects what is to be

---

* Machiavelli refers to the long tradition of advice books for princes, the *Speculum Principis* (Mirror of a Prince).

done for what should be done will learn how to bring about his ruin rather than his preservation. A man who always wishes to be good in every aspect among so many, who are not good, will be ruined. Therefore, it is necessary for a prince wishing to maintain his position to learn how not to be good and to use or not to use this knowledge according to necessity.

Putting aside imaginary things concerning princes and discussing what is real, I say that all men when they are spoken about (and especially princes, being more highly placed) are noted for those qualities which bring them either blame or praise. So someone may be considered liberal, another miserly, using the Tuscan term *misero*—because an avaricious person in our language, *avaro*, is someone who desires to possess by theft, while we call someone miserly who overly abstains from using what is his. So while one is considered generous, the other rapacious; one cruel, the other compassionate; one faithless, the other faithful; one effeminate and cowardly, the other fierce and brave; one humane, the other haughty; one lascivious, the other chaste; one sincere, the other cunning; one hard, the other easy; one severe, the other superficial; one religious, the other unbelieving, and so on. I know that everyone will claim that it would be most praiseworthy for a prince to exhibit all the above qualities that are considered good. Yet because they can neither be entirely possessed nor observed, for human nature does not permit it, it is necessary for him to be prudent enough to know how to avoid reproach for those vices which would lose him his state and to guard against those which might not, when possible. If he cannot, he can allow them to persist without too much concern. Again, he need not make himself uneasy about incurring reproach for those vices without which it is difficult to save the state, for if everything is considered carefully, it will be found that adhering to what appears to be a virtue will bring ruin; while adhering to something else that appears to be a vice will bring security and prosperity.

Chapter Sixteen

IT IS FINE [for a ruler] to be considered generous. Nevertheless, liberality exercised in such a way that you are considered liberal can harm you. However, if you use it skillfully and properly, so that it is inconspicuous; you will not run the risk of being accused of its opposite. Anyone wishing to maintain a reputation for generosity is obliged to not to leave out every sort of sumptuous display; so that a prince thus inclined will always consume all his resources in such acts, and will be compelled in the end, if he wishes to maintain a reputation for liberality, to unduly burden his people, to tax them and to do everything he can to get money. This will soon make his subjects hate him because once he is poor he will be of no value to anyone. Thus, due to his liberality, having offended many and rewarded few, he will notice every single difficulty and risk at the first danger. If he realizes this and wants to pull back, he immediately attracts the infamy of being called a miser.

Since a prince cannot display this virtue of liberality so that it is recognized as such in any way except to his own detriment; if he is prudent he should not worry about being called a miser, for in time he will actually be considered more and more liberal. When it is seen that because of his thriftiness, revenues suffice; he will be able to defend himself against anyone who wages war against him, and he will be able to embark on campaigns without burdening his people. So he will come to use liberality with everyone from whom he takes nothing (who are infinite in number) and be miserly with those few to whom he gives nothing.

We have not seen great deeds performed in our time except by those who were considered miserly; the rest have been defeated. Pope Julius II made use of his reputation for liberality in order to attain the papacy, yet in order to be able to wage war, he did not think to maintain it afterward. The present king of France [Louis XII] has conducted many wars without imposing any extra taxes on his subjects, because the additional expenses were offset by his long-standing thriftiness. The present king of Spain [Ferdinand II] would not have undertaken or succeeded in so many campaigns were he reputed to be liberal. Therefore, in order not to steal from his subjects, to be able to defend himself, not to become poor and despised, and not be forced to become rapacious, a prince should not worry about incurring a reputation as a miser, for it is one of those vices which will enable him to govern.

To anyone who says that Caesar obtained an empire by liberality, and that many others have reached the highest positions by having been liberal (or by being considered so), I answer: either you are already a prince or are on the road to becoming one. In the first case liberality is damaging; in the second it is actually quite necessary to be thought of as liberal. Caesar was one of those who wanted to become ruler of Rome; but if he had survived and had not moderated his expenses, he would have destroyed his government. And if anyone should reply that there have been many princes considered quite liberal who accomplished great military deeds, I reply that a prince either spends what is his own and his subjects', or else spends that of others. In the first case he should be thrifty; in the second he should always be liberal. The prince who goes out with his army and nourishes it by pillage, sackage, and extortion manages on what belongs to others. Such liberality is necessary for otherwise his soldiers would not follow. When it comes to what is neither yours nor your subjects', you can be a ready giver—as were Cyrus, Caesar, and Alexander—because spending what belongs to others does not harm your reputation, but enhances it. You only harm yourself by spending what is yours.*

There is nothing that consumes itself like liberality, for even while you exercise it you lose the power to do so, and thereby become either poor or despised— or else (in avoiding poverty) become rapacious and hated. Above all, a prince should guard against being despised and hated; and liberality leads you to both. Therefore, it is wiser to have a reputation as a miser, which brings reproach without hatred, than to be compelled to incur a name for rapacity by seeking a reputation for liberality, which produces reproach with hatred.

---

* The Persian emperor Cyrus II the Great (c. 580–c. 530 BCE), the Roman general and dictator Julius Caesar (100–44 BCE), the Macedonian king and conqueror Alexander the Great (356–323 BCE).

Chapter Seventeen

CONTINUING TO THE other qualities mentioned above, I say that every prince should desire to be considered merciful and not cruel. Nevertheless, he should take care not to misuse this clemency. Cesare Borgia was considered cruel but his cruelty brought order to Romagna, unified it, and restored it to peace and loyalty. If considered properly, one can see that he was much more merciful than the Florentine people, who, in order to avoid a reputation for cruelty, permitted the destruction of Pistoia. Therefore, as long as a prince keeps his subjects united and loyal, he should not worry about the infamy of a reputation for cruelty; because with a few examples he will be more merciful than those who, through excess mercy, allow disorders to arise, from which follow murders and robberies. These usually harm the entire population, while the executions that originate with a prince only harm a particular individual.

Here debate can arise on whether it is better to be loved than to be feared, or vice versa? The answer is that one would like to be both, but, because they are difficult to combine, it is much safer to be feared than loved, when one of the two must be discarded. Men are generally ungrateful and fickle, simulators and dissemblers; they flee in front of danger and are greedy for profit. As long as you act in their interests and do not need them, they are yours entirely; they will offer you their blood, property, life, and children. But, as I stated above, when the need approaches they turn against you. And any prince, who has founded himself entirely on their words and finds himself naked of other preparations, will be ruined. Friendships obtained by payment, and not greatness or nobility of spirit may be acquired but not owned, and in time of need cannot be spent. Men have fewer compunctions about offending someone who can make himself beloved than someone who can make himself feared, for love is held together by a link of obligation that, owing to the baseness of men, is broken at every opportunity for self interest; while fear is sustained by a dread of punishment that will never abandon you.

Nevertheless, a prince should make himself feared in such a way that if he does not acquire love, he avoids hatred. Being feared and not hated can go well together. This can always be achieved by abstaining from the property and the women of citizens and subjects. When it is necessary for him to proceed against someone's family, he must do it with proper justification and for an evident cause. But above all he must abstain from the property of others, because men more quickly forget the death of their father than the loss of their patrimony. Besides, there is never a lack of reasons to seize property, for he who begins to live through theft will always find a reason to take possession of others' belongings. On the other hand, reasons for acting against a family are more rare and fade sooner.

But when a prince is with his army and has a multitude of soldiers under his control, then it is necessary for him not to worry about incurring a reputation for cruelty, for without it he would never keep his army united or ready for combat.

Among the extraordinary deeds of Hannibal is that he had an enormous army, composed of an infinite variety of men whom he led to fight in foreign lands without any dissensions arising either among themselves or against the prince, no matter whether his fortunes were good or bad.* This could not have resulted

---

* The Carthaginian general Hannibal (247–183 BCE). Machiavelli wrote of the paradox regarding Hannibal and his adversary the Roman general Scipio Africanus the Elder (236–183 BCE). Both obtained remarkable results although their methods differed, with Scipio being known for his kindness and liberality, and Hannibal for his cruelty and ruthlessness.

from anything besides his inhuman cruelty, which, with his boundless abilities, made him a revered and terrifying presence before his soldiers. Without it, his other abilities would not have sufficed to attain the same effect.

On the question of being feared or loved, I conclude that men love at their pleasure and fear at the pleasure of the prince. A wise prince must found himself on what is his, not on what belongs to someone else. As was said, he must endeavor only to avoid hatred.

Chapter Eighteen

EVERYONE UNDERSTANDS HOW praiseworthy it is for a prince to keep his word and to
live by integrity, not by deceit. Nevertheless,
one may see from the experience of our times that
those princes who accomplished great deeds paid little attention to keeping promises. They knew how to
deceive the minds of men with astuteness, and in the
end were able to prevail over those who based themselves on loyalty. You must therefore understand that
there are two ways to fight: one by laws, the other by
force. The first method is unique to men, the second
to beasts; but because the first is frequently insuffi-
cient, it is necessary to have recourse to the second.
Therefore, it is necessary for a prince to understand
how to behave both like a beast and like a man.

Since a prince needs to know how to behave like
a beast, he should take from the fox and the lion;

because the lion has no defense against traps, and the fox has no defense against wolves.* Therefore, it is necessary to be a fox to recognize traps and a lion to scare away wolves. Those who play only the part of the lion do not understand this. Therefore, a wise lord cannot and should not keep his word when its observance may be turned against him, and when the reasons that caused him to pledge it no longer exist. If men were entirely good this precept would not hold, but because they are a sad lot, and will not keep faith with you, you do not have to keep it with them. Nor has any prince ever lacked legitimate reasons to disguise a non-observance. Of this, endless modern examples could be given, showing how many treaties and promises have been violated and made void through the faithlessness of princes. He who has known best how to act the fox has succeeded best.

But it is necessary to know how to disguise this ability and to be a great pretender and dissembler; for men are so simple, and so controlled by immediate concerns, that he who seeks to deceive will always find someone willing to be deceived. There is one recent example that I cannot pass over in silence. [Pope] Alexander VI never did anything nor did he ever think of anything besides deceiving men; and

---

* In addition to the fable by the Greek writer Aesop, a possible source for Machiavelli was *officiis* (I, 13) by the Roman orator Marcus Tullius Cicero (106–43 BCE).

he always found a subject on whom to practice. For there never was a man more convincing in his assertions and who swore to something more fervently who kept his word less. Nevertheless, his deceits always followed his vows, because he understood this aspect of the world so well.

Therefore, while it is not necessary for a prince to have all the good qualities I have listed above, it is quite necessary to appear to have them. And I dare say this as well, that to have them and to always observe them is harmful, but to appear to have them is useful. So he must appear to be truly merciful, faithful, humane, religious, upright, but his mind must always be ready to transform itself into the opposite.

It is necessary for a prince, especially a new prince, not to respect all those things for which men are esteemed, being often forced—in order to maintain the state—to act contrary to fidelity, charity, humanity, and religion. Therefore, it is necessary for him to have a mind ready to change as the winds of Fortune and the variety of events command, yet, as I have said above, not to diverge from the good if possible, but to know how to enter into evil when needed.

A prince must be very careful to never to let anything come out of his mouth that is not replete with the above-named five qualities, so that he may appear to anyone who sees and hears him as entirely merciful, faithful, honest, upright, and religious. There is nothing more necessary than to appear to have this last quality, since men judge generally more with their eyes than with their hands, because everyone can see but few get to touch. Everyone sees what you appear to be; few get to touch what you are, and those few dare not oppose the opinion of so many who have the majesty of the state to defend them. In the actions of all men and especially of princes where there is no court for appeals, one looks at the ends.* As long as a prince can win and maintain his state, the means will always be judged as honorable and praiseworthy by everybody; because the common people are always swayed by appearances and by results; and if the world is anything, it is common. The elite may find their place when the masses have something they can rely upon.

One contemporary prince,[†] whom it is not well to name, never preaches anything but peace and faith, yet he is the absolute enemy of one and the other, for if he had kept to one or the other he would have been relieved of his reputation and kingdom many times over.

---

* This sentence and the one following are a likely source for the aphorism "The ends justify the means," often identified with Machiavelli.

† Ferdinand II of Aragon.

Chapter Nineteen

WITH REGARDS TO the characteristics mentioned above, I have spoken about the most important. I now wish to briefly discuss the others according to the following generalizations—that the prince must understand, as was partly stated above, how to avoid what can make him hated and contemptible; for when he avoids this, he will have done his part, and will find no danger in other infamies.

As I have said, what makes him hated above all is to be rapacious and abusive of the women and property of his subjects, from these he must abstain. The majority of men live contentedly as long as neither their property nor their honor is taken away. Then one has only to contend with the ambitions of a small minority who can easily be restrained in many ways.

What makes him contemptible is to be considered fickle, frivolous, effeminate, pusillanimous, irresolute, from which a prince should guard himself as from a reef. He should endeavor that his actions be recognized for their greatness, energy, gravity, and fortitude; and in his private dealings with his subjects let him insist that his rulings are irrevocable in order to establish the sort of reputation where no one would think of deceiving him or cheating him.

A prince who conveys such an impression of himself will be highly esteemed, and it is difficult to conspire and attack someone with such a reputation, since his excellence is understood and he is revered by his people.

One of the most efficient safeguards a prince can have against conspiracies is not to be hated and despised by the masses, for he who conspires always believes he will satisfy the people with the death of the prince; but when the conspirator believes he might anger them, he will not have the courage to perform such an act, for the difficulties facing conspirators are infinite. Experience demonstrates that there have been many conspiracies, but few have been successful because he who conspires cannot act alone; nor can he take a companion except from those whom he believes to be malcontents, and as soon as you have revealed your intentions to a malcontent you have given him the means to content himself because he can hope for every advantage. Seeing certain gain on one side, and with the other side doubtful and full of danger, to keep faith with you he must be either an exceptional friend or a thoroughly committed enemy of the prince.

Therefore, I say that, on the side of the conspirator, there is nothing but fear, jealousy, and the prospect of punishment to terrify him; but on the side of the prince there is the majesty of the principality, the laws, the protection of friends and the state to defend him; so that, if added to all these things is popular goodwill, it is impossible that anyone will have the temerity to conspire. Usually a conspirator has to be afraid before committing his evil deed, but in this case he has also to fear the aftermath, for with the people as an enemy he cannot hope to find any refuge at all.

Princes should leave unpopular duties to the management of others and keep the popular ones for themselves and respect the elite but not make themselves hated by the people.

Here it must be noted that hatred is acquired as much by good works as by bad ones; therefore, as I said above, a prince who wants to maintain his state is very often forced not to be good. When the group you deem most necessary to keeping your position is corrupt—be it the people or the soldiers or the elite—it is in your interests to follow their whims to their satisfaction and then good works can be your enemy.

Let us consider [the Roman Emperor] Alexander,* who was of such goodness, that among other praise he received is that in the fourteen years he held the empire he put no one to death without trial. Nevertheless, since he was considered effeminate and allowed himself to be ruled by his mother, he came to be despised, and the army conspired against him and murdered him.

In contrast [to Alexander] were the qualities of Commodus, Severus, Antoninus Caracalla, and Maximinus.† You will find that they were all extremely cruel and rapacious men who in order to satisfy their soldiers did not hesitate to commit every sort of injury possible against the people. And all, except Severus, ended badly. Severus had such ability that even though he oppressed the people, he retained the friendship of the military and reigned successfully. His virtues were so admired by the soldiers and people that the latter remained astonished and awed, and the former were respectful and satisfied. Because the actions of this man, as a new prince, were so great and noteworthy, I wish to show briefly how well he understood to use the character of both the fox and the lion, whose natures, as I said above, a prince must imitate.

---

* Roman emperor Alexander Severus (209–235).

† Roman emperors: Commodus (161–192), Septimius Severus (145–211), Caracalla (188–217), Gaius Julius Verus Maximinus (173–238).

Knowing the indolence of the Emperor Julian, Severus persuaded the army he commanded in Slavonia that it would be right to go to Rome and avenge the death of Pertinax, who had been put to death by the Praetorian Guard.* Under this pretext, and without appearing to aspire to the empire, he moved the army on Rome and reached Italy before it was known that he had departed. Upon his arrival at Rome, the Senate elected him emperor out of fear, and Julian was put to death. After this beginning, Severus, who wanted to make himself master of the entire state, still faced two obstacles: one in Asia, where Niger, head of the army in Asia, had himself proclaimed emperor; the other in the West, where Albinus† also aspired to the empire. Since he judged it dangerous to reveal that he was an enemy of both, he decided to attack Niger and to deceive Albinus by writing that having been elected emperor by the Senate he wanted to share that dignity with him. He sent him the title of Caesar and assured that by senatorial decree Albinus would become his colleague. Albinus accepted all of this as true. But after Severus had settled affairs in the East by conquering and killing Niger, he returned to Rome and made charges in the Senate that Albinus had not been grateful for the benefits received and

---

* Roman emperors Flavius Claudius Julianus "the Apostate" (331/332–363), Publius Helvius Pertinax (126–193).

† Roman general Albinus (150–197).

had treacherously sought to murder him, and for this ingratitude he was compelled to punish him. Afterward, he sought him out in France and took from him both his position and his life. Anyone who carefully examines the actions of this man will find in him a most fierce lion and a most cunning fox; and will see that he was feared and respected by everyone, and not hated by the army. One should not be surprised that he, a new man, was able to hold the empire so well, because his great reputation always protected him from the hatred that his plundering might have produced among the people.

His son Antoninus* was also a man of great qualities, which made him admirable in the sight of the people and acceptable to the soldiers, for he was a military man able to endure the greatest fatigue. He despised all delicate food and soft living, which made him beloved by the army. Nevertheless, his ferocity and cruelty were so great and so unheard of that by having committed countless homicides he killed a large part of the population of Rome and all that of Alexandria. He thus became hated by the whole world, and was so feared by those around him that he was murdered in the middle of his army by a centurion. Here it must be noted that a death deliberately inflicted by a determined individual cannot

---

* Roman emperor Caracalla.

be avoided by princes, because someone who does not care about dying can always harm him; but a prince would do well not to fear too much on this account, for it is quite rare. He does have to refrain from inflicting serious harm on those he keeps nearby in the service of his government like Antoninus. By shamefully putting to death a brother of that centurion, threatening him daily yet still keeping him in his bodyguard, Antoninus made a rash decision that could ruin him—as in fact happened.

But let us come to Commodus, someone who should have held the empire easily, since he inherited it as the son of Marcus Aurelius. It would have been enough for him to satisfy the people and the army by following in his father's footsteps; but, being of a cruel and bestial disposition, in order to exercise his rapacity on the people, he turned to entertaining the soldiers and corrupting them. On the other hand, he did not maintain his dignity, often descending into the arena to fight with gladiators and doing other vile things unworthy of the imperial majesty, and so he became contemptible to the soldiers. Being hated by one party and despised by the other, he was conspired against and put to death.

It remains to discuss the qualities of Maximinus, an extremely warlike man. The army, disgusted by the soft living of Alexander, put him to death and elected Maximinus to the empire. But he did not possess it for long, as two things made him hated and contemptible. One was his base origin as a sheepherder in Thrace, which brought him into contempt (it became known everywhere and aroused universal indignation); the other was that at the outset of his reign he delayed going to Rome in order to claim the imperial throne. He also gained a reputation for the utmost ferocity by committing many acts of cruelty through his prefects in Rome and elsewhere in the empire. Thus the whole world was moved to disdain the baseness of his blood and to fear his ferocity. First Africa rebelled, and then the Senate with all the people of Rome, and all Italy conspired against him. Added to this was his own army encamped at Aquileia. Finding it difficult to capture and annoyed by his cruelty, the soldiers came to fear him less (once he had so many enemies), so they murdered him.

Chapter Twenty

Our forefathers, and those who were considered wise, would state that it was necessary to hold Pistoia with factions and Pisa with fortresses; with this in mind, they encouraged discord in some of their subject towns in order to retain possession more easily. This may have been well enough in times when there was a balance of power in Italy, but I do not believe that it can be used as a rule today. I do not believe that factions ever do any good; on the contrary, when the enemy approaches divided cities are certain to be lost immediately, because the weaker faction will always join with the outside forces and the other will not be able to hold out. I believe the Venetians were moved by the reasoning above to encourage the Guelph and Ghibelline factions in their subject cities; and although they never allowed them to come to bloodshed, they did encourage disputes between them so that the citizens, distracted by their differences, would not unite against them. As has been seen, this did not work in their favor because, after the rout at Vailà, one faction immediately took courage and seized the entire state.* Such methods reveal the weakness of a prince. In a strong principality such divisions are never allowed, as they are useful only in peacetime, enabling one to more easily manage subjects; but when war comes, this policy reveals its defects.

Princes, especially new ones, have found more loyalty and utility in those men who at the beginning of their rule were suspect than among those who in the beginning were trusted. Pandolfo Petrucci, prince of Siena, ruled his state more by those who had been suspect than by others. On this question one cannot speak generally, for it varies so much by case; I will say only this, that a prince may gain with the greatest ease anyone who at the beginning of the principality was hostile. They will need support in order to maintain themselves and will be forced to serve him faithfully, since they realize that they must erase with deeds the bad impression the prince has of them. Thus the prince will always extract more profit from them than from those who are so comfortable in his service that they might neglect his interests. And since the sub-

---

* In 1509 at Agnadello the French under Louis XI defeated a Venetian army.

ject requires it, I do not wish to fail to warn princes who have recently acquired a state, thanks to the aid of its inhabitants, to carefully consider the motives that spurred those citizens to help them. If it is not due to some natural affection for him on their part but only because they were dissatisfied with the previous state, then he will be able to retain their friendship only with great effort and difficulty, for it will be impossible for him to satisfy them. Examination of precedents taken from ancient and modern events reveals that it is easier for the prince to make friends among those men who were content under the former state, and therefore were his enemies, than among those who became his allies out of dissatisfaction and helped him to occupy it.

In order to secure their states, it has been a custom with princes to erect fortresses that may serve as bit and bridle to those plotting something against them, and as places of refuge from an unexpected attack.

Fortresses, therefore, are useful or not according to circumstances; if they benefit you in one way, they may harm you in another. A prince who has more to fear from the people than from foreigners should build fortresses, but he who has more to fear from foreigners than from the people can do without them. The castle of Milan, built by Francesco Sforza, has caused and will cause more wars against the house of Sforza than any other disorder in the state. Not being hated by the people is the best possible fortress, because even if you have fortresses, they will not save you if the people hate you; if the people take up arms, there will never be a lack of foreigners to help them. In our times fortresses have not been useful to any prince except the Countess of Forli;* when her husband, Count Girolamo, was killed she was able to flee the attack of the people, await help from Milan, and regain her state. During that period there were no foreigners able to help the people. But fortresses were of little value afterward when Cesare Borgia attacked, and her enemy, the people, joined with the foreigners. Therefore, it would have been safer for her on both occasions not to be hated by the people than to have fortresses. Having considered all these things, I shall praise anyone who builds fortresses as well as anyone who does not, but I will criticize whoever puts their trust in fortresses and cares little about being hated by the people.

---

* Caterina Sforza (1463–1509).

Chapter Twenty-One

NOTHING BRINGS A prince so much esteem as great enterprises and setting a fine example. We have in our time Ferdinand of Aragon, the present king of Spain. He can almost be called a new prince, because he has risen, by fame and glory, from being a weak king to become the foremost king in Christendom; and if you will consider his deeds, you will find them all great and some extraordinary. In the beginning of his reign he attacked Granada; this enterprise was the foundation of his state. First, he acted at his leisure and without fear of opposition, for he busied the minds of the barons of Castile with thoughts of the war rather than in anticipation of innovations; by this means he acquired power and authority over them without their realizing it. During that long war he was able to sustain his armies with the money from the Church and the people, and lay the foundation for his own army which has since distinguished him. Furthermore, in order to undertake even greater enterprises he always used religion and behaved with sanctimonious cruelty, plundering and driving the Marranos* from his kingdom. There could be no example more miserable or unusual. Under this same guise he attacked Africa, undertook the campaign in Italy, and has recently attacked France. He has always planned and performed great deeds that have kept the minds of his subjects in suspense and full of admiration. And his actions are born one from another, never allowing any space between one event and the next for men to calmly proceed against him.

A prince is also respected when he is either a true friend or a true enemy: that is, when, without reservation, he declares himself in favor of someone and against someone else. Such a policy is always more profitable than remaining neutral, because if two powerful neighbors come to blows, their characteristics are such that if one of them wins, you have either to fear the victor or not. In either of these situations it will always be more profitable to declare yourself and wage a good war effort; in the first case, if you do not declare yourself, you will invariably fall prey to the winner, to the pleasure and satisfaction of the

---

* The term "Marrano" is a pejorative term for Jews and Muslims who converted to Christianity.

vanquished, and you will have no argument in your defense or anything to assist you. Whoever wins will not want unreliable friends unwilling to aid him in times of adversity; and whoever loses will not assist you because you were unwilling to take up arms and share in his fortunes.

A prince should never make an alliance with someone more powerful than himself in order to injure others, unless compelled by necessity; because in victory you remain under their power, and princes should avoid, whenever possible, any situation in which they are at someone else's discretion.

No state should ever believe that it can choose a perfectly safe course of action; rather, let it regard all choices as dubious, because it is in the nature of things to find that you can never avoid one trouble without running into another, and prudence consists in being able to distinguish between the types of trouble, and treat the lesser evil as something good.

A prince ought also to demonstrate that he is a lover of virtue who honors and supports virtuous men and excellent artists. At the same time, he should encourage his citizens to practice their callings peaceably—in commerce, agriculture, and every other human activity—so that nobody should be afraid of improving their property out of fear that it will be taken away from him or from starting a business out of fear of taxes; instead he should reward anyone who would do such things or anything else that could develop his city and state.

He should also entertain the people with festivals and spectacles at appropriate times of the year; and as every city is divided into guilds or into groups, he should hold such bodies in esteem, associate with them sometimes and show himself as an example of humanity and munificence—always maintaining the dignity of his station.

Chapter Twenty-Two

THE CHOICE OF ministers is of no little importance to a prince, and they are either good or not according to the prudence of the prince. The first impression that one forms of a prince's brains is by observing the men around him; when they are capable and faithful, he may always be considered wise, because he has known how to recognize the capable and to keep them faithful. But when they are otherwise, one cannot form a good opinion of him.

There is a method that never fails for a prince to know his ministers; when you see the minister thinking more of himself than of you, and seeking his personal profit in everything, such a man will never make a good minister, nor will you ever be able to trust him; because anyone who has the state of another in his hands should never think of himself but always of his prince, and never pay any attention to matters that do not concern the prince.

Chapter Twenty-Three

I DO NOT WISH to leave out an important point regarding a mistake princes have difficulty avoiding unless they are quite prudent and discriminating. These are the flatterers that fill the courts. Because men take so much pleasure in their personal affairs, to the point of self-deception, they have difficulty defending themselves from this plague. He who wants to protect himself runs the risk of being despised because there is no other way to guard oneself against flattery than by letting it be known that telling the truth will not offend you; but if anyone can tell you the truth, you will no longer be held in respect.

Therefore, a prudent prince should take a third course by choosing wise men for his state and giving only them the liberty to speak the truth to him, and then only regarding his inquiries, and nothing else. But he should question them about everything and listen to their opinions, and then decide for himself, on his own. With these counsels and with each advisor he should carry himself in such a way that each of them should know that that the more freely one speaks, the more he will be welcomed; beyond this, he should not listen to anyone. He should instead follow and remain steadfast on a decision once taken. For anyone who does otherwise, either the flatterers will be his downfall, or he will lose prestige by changing opinions so often.

A prince, therefore, should always seek counsel, but only when he wishes and not when someone else wishes it; he should actually discourage anyone from offering advice unless he asks for it. But he should make constant inquiries and afterward listen with patience concerning the truth about whatever was inquired about; and he should get angry if he learns that someone for whatever reason will not speak to him.

There are some who deceive themselves into thinking that a prince who conveys an impression of prudence does so not because of his own ability, but because of the good advisers he has about him. A general rule that never fails is that a prince who is not wise himself will never take good advice, unless by chance he has yielded his affairs entirely to one person who happens to be a very prudent man. In this case he may do well, but not for long, because such a governor would in a short time take the state away from him.

Thus, by receiving the advice of more than one, an unwise prince will never have counselors who can work together, and he will not be able to unite them on his own. For each counselor will think of his own interests and the prince will not be able to control them or even understand them. And things cannot proceed in any other way, for men will always serve you poorly unless necessity makes them behave well. Therefore, it can be concluded that good advice, no matter whence it comes, must be born from the wisdom of the prince, rather than the wisdom of the prince from good advice.

Chapter Twenty-Four

THE PREVIOUS SUGGESTIONS, carefully observed, will enable a new prince to appear well established, and render him at once more secure and stable in a state than if he had been long seated there. This is because the actions of a new prince are observed much more than those of a hereditary one, and when they are seen to be capable, they gain hold over men and obligate them more than ancient blood. Men are attracted more by the present than by the past, and when they find the present good, they enjoy it and seek nothing else. They will also do anything to defend a prince who does not fail them in other things. Thus he will have double the glory by establishing a new principality, adorning and strengthening it with good laws, good arms, good allies, and with good examples; as he will have double the disgrace, born a prince by losing his state due to a lack of prudence.

These princes of ours who held their principalities for so many years must not blame Fortune because they lost them but rather their own ineptitude, since it never occurred to them during tranquil times that things could change (it is a common defect of men not to prepare for a storm in good weather). Afterward, when bad times came, they thought of flight instead of defending themselves. They hoped that the people, disgusted by the insolence of the conquerors, would call them back. If there were no alternatives this would be a good tactic, but it is really terrible to have acted this way only because other solutions were neglected. One should never accept the idea of falling because someone will be there to catch you: either it will not happen; or if it does happen, you have no guarantees with such a cowardly form of defense that does not depend on you. The only forms of defense that are good, reliable, and lasting are those in which you rely on yourself and on your own abilities.

Chapter Twenty-Five

I T IS NOT unknown to me that many men have held, and still hold, the opinion that the affairs of the world are so thoroughly ruled by Fortune and by God that human prudence cannot, control them. And for this they might conclude that there is no need to sweat over anything, but rather allow oneself to be ruled by fate. This opinion has gained credence in our times because of the great changes that have been seen and can still be observed every day beyond all human capacity for understanding. Sometimes in pondering this, I am inclined to join their opinion. Nevertheless, as long as our free will is not extinguished, I hold it to be true that Fortune is the arbiter of one-half of our actions, but that she still allows us to rule the other half (or thereabouts).

I compare her to one of those raging rivers that overflows the plains, destroying trees and buildings,

moving the soil from place to place. Everything flees before them and yields to their impetus, unable to resist them in any way. And yet, although that is how they are, it does not mean that when the weather is calm that men cannot make some provision with barriers and dikes so that when the rivers rise again, they can be diverted into canals. That way, their onslaught will not be so unruly and damaging.*
Something similar happens with Fortune, which shows all her power where there is no organized ability to resist her; for that is where she directs her fury, where she knows that no dikes and shelters have been raised to contain her.

And if you think about Italy, which is the center and the cause of these changes, you will see a country without any dikes or barriers, for if she were protected with commensurate ability, either this flood would not have caused the great changes it has wrought or it would not have arrived at all.

I do not want to add anything more about resisting Fortune in general, but in limiting myself to more particular cases, I say that it may be seen how different men behave differently in order to reach the goals they seek: namely wealth and glory. One might

---

* A section which reveals the possible influence of the Roman philosopher Lucretius (99–55 BCE) and the *De rerum natura* (*On the Nature of Things*) V, 261–272. There is evidence that Machiavelli is the author of a transcription of Lucretius in the *Codex Vaticanus* 884.

be cautious, another impetuous; one may use force, another skill; one may be patient, another the opposite; and each may succeed though using different methods. One can also see that with two cautious men, one may attain his goal and the other will not.

Success depends on the ability to change course, for someone who behaves cautiously and patiently in a period when such behavior is rewarded could be ruined if he does not change his procedure as times and circumstances change. It is not possible to find a man who is so wise that he knows when to adapt because men cannot deviate from their natural inclinations and because one cannot be persuaded to leave a path that has always brought prosperity. Therefore, when the time for impetuous action arrives, a cautious man does not know what to do, and that is his downfall. If one could change inclination with the times and circumstances, then fortune would never change.

Pope Julius II acted impetuously in everything and found that way of proceeding so well suited to the times and circumstances that he always achieved a happy end. Consider his first enterprise against Bologna, when Messer Giovanni Bentivogli was still alive. The Venetians were not happy about it, nor was the king of Spain (he was still in negotiations with France). Nevertheless, Julius personally led the expedition with aggressiveness and impetuosity. This move disturbed and paralyzed the king of Spain and the Venetians, the latter out of fear, the king due to his desire to regain the entire kingdom of Naples. On the other side the pope dragged along the king of France, who after seeing the pope make such a move, wanted to earn his friendship in order to put down the Venetians and reasoned that he could not deny him troops without blatantly offending him. With this impetuous action, Julius accomplished what no other pontiff could ever have done with all of their human prudence; for had he waited for all of the negotiations to be settled and everything to be in order before leaving Rome, as most any other pontiff would have done, he would have never succeeded. The king of France would have made a thousand excuses, and the others would have raised a thousand fears.

I will leave aside Julius's other actions, as they were all alike, and they all succeeded, for the shortness of his life meant he never experienced a reversal. However, had times arrived that required proceeding with caution, it would have resulted in his downfall, for he would never have deviated from the method that suited his nature.

I conclude, therefore, that, since Fortune varies and since men are set in their ways, men will be successful when they act in accordance with Fortune and unsuccessful with they do not. For my part, I reason that it is better to be impetuous than cautious, because Fortune is a woman, and if you wish to make her submit it is necessary to beat and abuse her. She allows herself to be won over by the impetuous rather than by those who behave coldly. As a woman, she is a friend of the young, for they are less cautious, more ferocious, and can command her with more audacity.

Chapter Twenty-Six

HAVING CAREFULLY CONSIDERED everything mentioned above, I have asked myself whether the present times and circumstances in Italy would be propitious to honor a new prince; and I cannot think of another time more suited than the present.

If it was necessary for the people of Israel to be enslaved in Egypt in order to recognize the ability of Moses, for the Persians to be oppressed by the Medes to discover the greatness of spirit of Cyrus, and for the Athenians to be dispersed for the excellence of Theseus; then at the present time, in order to discover the ability of the Italian spirit, it has been necessary for Italy to be reduced to her present condition: more enslaved than the Hebrews, more oppressed than the Persians, more scattered than the Athenians; without a leader, without order, beaten, despoiled, torn, over-run; enduring every form of ruin.

Although before now there have been glimmers of hope that someone might lead us to believe that he was ordained by God for the redemption of Italy, nevertheless as seen afterward, Fortune rejected him at the highest point of his actions. Now almost life-less, Italy awaits the one who can heal her wounds and put an end to the sacking of Lombardy, the extortion of the kingdom* and Tuscany, and cure the sores that have been festering for so long. Look how she prays God to send someone to deliver her from this barbaric cruelty and insolence. Look how ready she is to follow a standard as long as there is someone to raise it. There is no one in sight in whom she can hope more to lead this redemption than your illustrious house,† with its virtue and fortune, favored by God and by the Church, over which it now prince. It will not be so difficult if you keep in mind the actions and lives of the men described above. Although they are indeed rare and marvelous, they were still men, each of them acted in circumstances less favorable than the present, and their enterprises were no more just nor easier, nor was God more their friend than yours.

---

* The kingdom of Naples.

† The house in question is the Medici and Giovanni de' Medici (1475–1521) elected Pope Leo X in 1513.

The opportunity for Italy to finally behold her redeemer must not be allowed to pass. How can I express with what love he would be received in all the provinces that have suffered so much from this flood of foreigners: what thirst for revenge, what earnest faith, what devotion, what tears? What door would be closed to him? What people would deny him obedience? What envy would hinder him? What Italian would refuse him homage? This barbarian dominance stinks to everyone. Let your illustrious house grasp this mission with the courage and hope that are party to a just cause, so that under its standard our fatherland may be ennobled, and under its auspices Petrarch's exhortation may come to pass:

> Virtue against fury shall advance the fight,
> And it i' th' combat soon shall put to flight:
> For the old Roman valor is not dead,
> Nor in th' Italians' breasts extinguished.*

---

* Petrarch, Francesco Petrarca (1304–1374), *Italia mia* (II, 93–96).

Letter from Niccolò Machiavelli to Francesco Vettori

Florence; December 10, 1513

To the Magnificent Francesco Vettori, Florentine ambassador to the Supreme Pontiff, His Patron and Benefactor. Rome.

Magnificent Ambassador. "Divine favor was never tardy."* This I say because I seem to have lost, or rather misplaced, your favor, as it has been such a long time since you wrote to me that I wondered what might be the reason. I paid scant attention to most explanations that came to mind, except perhaps you have not written because you received word that I was not a good steward of your letters. I know that besides Filippo

---

* Francesco Petrarch, *Triumph of Eternity*, 13.

and Pagolo, no one else has seen them because of me.*
I am reassured by your letter of the 23rd of last month
and am very happy to see how skillfully and calmly
you are performing your public duties. I urge you to
continue to do so, because whoever neglects his own
needs for others loses his own and receives no recognition thereby. Since Fortune wants to control everything and wants to be allowed to do so, remain calm,
don't bother her, and wait until she allows men something. That will be the time to make an effort, to be
more attentive, and that will also be the time for me
to leave my farm and announce, "Here I am." Because
I want to reciprocate fully, in this letter I will only tell
you about how my life is going. If you judge it worth
exchanging for yours, I will gladly make the trade.

Since the latest events, I have been staying on the
farm, not spending more than twenty days in Florence. I have been catching thrushes by hand, getting up
before daybreak, preparing the birdlime, and going out
with a stack of cages looking like Geta returning from
the port with Amphitryon's books.[†] I usually catch a
couple of thrushes, six at most. That is how I spent Sep-
tember. My life is such that when this nasty and weird
pastime came to an end, I actually missed it. I still get
up with the sun and go for a couple of hours into one of

---

* F. Casavecchia and P. Vettori.

† *Geta and Birria* by Domenico da Prato.

my woods I am having cut down. I stay for a couple of hours to check the previous day's work and spend some time with the woodcutters, who always have some disaster at hand among themselves or with some neighbors. I could tell a thousand tales about these woods and Frosino da Panzano and others who wanted some firewood. Frosino in particular sent for a load without notifying me, and when it was time to pay, he wanted to withhold ten lire, claiming he had won it off me four years ago in a game of *cricca** at Antonio Guicciardini's house. I started raising hell and wanted to accuse the wagoneer of being a thief, but Giovanni Machiavelli stepped in and we came to an agreement. Then Battista Guicciardini, Filippo Ginori, Tommaso del Bene, and some other citizens each ordered a load as the north wind began to blow. I made promises to each of them and sent one load to Tommaso in Florence, but it turned into a half load the way he, his wife, children, and servants stacked it. They looked like Gaburra on Thursdays when he and his boys are whacking an ox. When I realized who was actually making a profit, I told the others that I was out of wood, and they all flew off the handle—especially Battista, who includes this among the other catastrophes from Prato.[†]

---

* A card game.

† Prato, a city outside Florence, was sacked in 1512 by Spanish troops who routed a militia organized by Machiavelli, paving the way for the restoration of the Medici regime.

After I leave the woods, I go to a spring and then to one of my bird lairs. I have a book under my arm: either Dante or Petrarch, or one of the lesser poets like Tibullus, Ovid, or the like. I read about their love affairs and remember my own. These thoughts keep me happy for a while. Then I take the road toward the inn and chat with passersby, asking for news about their countries, learning about things, and considering the variety of habits and fancies of men. Then comes time to eat, and with my household I partake of the foods that this small farm and miniscule patrimony allow. After I have eaten, I go back to the inn, where there is usually the innkeeper, a butcher, a miller, and a couple of bakers. I hang around with them the rest of the day, playing *cricca* and backgammon, games that lead to a thousand arguments and endless harsh insults. Even though we usually argue over a pittance, you can hear our shouts all the way to San Casciano. At least being stuck with these louts gets the dust and mold out of my brain and helps vent the spite over my fate. I could accept being downtrodden in this manner if I could see that Fate had any shame about treating me so.

When evening comes, I return home and enter my study. At the threshold I remove my daily outfit, full of dirt and mud, and put on my regal and priestly attire. When I am appropriately dressed, I enter the hallowed halls of the ancients, where I am welcomed and nourished on that food which is mine alone, and for which I was born. I am not ashamed to converse and query with them about the motivations for their exploits. They respond with such humane dignity that for four hours I feel no boredom, forget all my travails, and no longer fear poverty; nor am I terrified by death. My entire being communes with them. Since Dante states that learning does not occur without retention, I make notes to retain the capital earned from these conversations and have composed a brief treatise, *De principatibus* [*On Principalities*], in which I delve deeply into the ideas of the topic, examining the very definition of a princely realm, the categories, how they are attained and maintained, and why they are lost. If any of my notions has ever pleased you, this one should please you all the more. A prince—and especially a new prince—should welcome it. Therefore I am dedicating it to His Magnificence Giuliano.* Filippo da Casavecchia has seen it and can provide you with more details about the work and our discussions although I am still adding to it and cleaning it up.

Magnificent Ambassador, you have encouraged me to leave this life and come to enjoy yours with you. I will do so eventually, but presently certain

---

* The death of Giuliano de' Medici (1479–1516) caused Machiavelli to change the dedication to Lorenzo de' Medici (1492–1519).

commitments here require my attention, which should be resolved in six weeks time. What causes me some concern are the Soderinis, who are also in Rome. Were I to come down, I would be obliged to visit and speak with them.* Upon my return home I might not get to dismount at home but at the Bargello.† For even if the present regime has a strong foundation and seems secure, it is still newly established and therefore suspicious. There are many knivers like Pagolo Bertini, out to make a name for themselves, who would put others out to dry and leave me with the tab. I entreat you to calm this fear of mine; then, come what may, I will visit you at the said time.

I discussed with Filippo whether or not it would be a good idea to give this little treatise of mine to him [Giuliano]. And if it is a good idea, whether I should present it myself or send it to you. If I do not present it, I wonder whether Giuliano will ever read it and whether Ardighelli will take credit for this latest effort of mine. In favor of sending it is my present state of need because I am wasting away here and cannot remain like this much longer without becoming despicably poor. There is also my desire that these Medici lords might be able to use me even if it were

---

* Piero Soderini (1450–1522), leader of the Florentine republic in which Machiavelli was a functionary. A meeting with Soderini would have raised suspicions in Medici circles.

† The Bargello was a prison in Florence.

just to have me roll a stone. If I cannot win them over, I have only myself to blame. This study of mine, if it were ever to be read, would make it clear that for fifteen years I have been studying the art of statecraft and not sleeping or playing around, and anyone would value the services of someone who has gained so much experience at others' expense. There should be no doubt about my good faith, for I have always kept my word. Anyone like me, who has been faithful and good for forty-three years, cannot change their disposition, as my poverty can surely attest. I would hope that you will also write to me about these matters. I commend myself to you. Be happy.

December 10, 1513
Niccolò Machiavelli, Florence

Index